All rights reserved. International copyright secured.
No part of this book may be reproduced, stored in a retrieval system, or transmitted in any form or by any means—electronic, mechanical, photocopying, recording, or otherwise—without the prior written permission of Learning Engineered Publishing, a division Learning Engineered LLC except for inclusion of brief quotations in an acknowledged review.

Title: *God's Love in Every Pattern*
Subtitle: *A Journey Through God's Beautiful World*
Written by: Christian A. Dickinson

Illustrations by: Learning Engineered LLC
Published by: Learning Engineered Publishing, [https://learningengineeredpublishing.com/]

Library of Congress Control Number: 2025944123
ISBN (Print): 978-1-965741-44-3

First Edition: 2025

Printed & Created in: United States of America
Text and Illustration Copyright © 2025

Adapted from the book *The Unseen Pattern: God's Rhythms in Time, Beauty, and the Gospel* by Christian A. Dickinson.

One or more illustrations in this book may have been created, altered, or edited using AI-assisted tools.

Learning Engineered Publishing is a division of Learning Engineered LLC and a subsidiary of Carpe Diem Unlimited Holdings, Inc.

DEDICATION

For my son, MCD

GOD'S PATTERNS

God's world is full of patterns,

big and small,

Sunrises, spirals—

His love in them all!

Jesus weaves His care

in ways so clear,

Find His patterns—

they draw us near!

God's patterns show His love.

Jesus, help me see Your patterns!

SUNRISES

Every sunrise glows with

God's bright care,

Painting the sky with colors rare.

Jesus is the Light,

shining each day,

His promise of hope

won't fade away!

God's hope shines like the sun.

What colors do you see in a sunrise?

HEARTBEATS

Your heart goes thump,

a beat so strong,

God made it sing His steady song.

Jesus holds your heart

with gentle care,

His love beats steady,

always there!

God loves your heart.

Thank You, Jesus, for my heartbeat!

COMMUNITY

Friends and family share

God's love so wide,

Like neighbors helping side by side.

Jesus joins us with

His friendship true,

His care makes our

hearts renew!

God's love grows with friends.

Who's a friend who shows God's love?

MUSIC

Birds and waves sing

God's sweet tune,

His music dances morning to noon!

Jesus loves our songs,

so glad and free,

Sing His joy for all to see!

God's joy is a song.

Jesus, help me sing Your joy!

SPIRALS

Spirals in shells and
flowers twirl round,
God's lovely patterns
are easily found!
Jesus made them perfect,
swirling bright,
Each spiral shows
His love and light.

God makes beautiful things.
Thank You, Jesus, for spirals!

FLOWERS

Flowers bloom in patterns,

oh so neat,

Petals spinning,

a God-made treat!

Jesus paints them lovely,

blooming for you,

His beauty grows in all things true.

God's beauty is in flowers.

What's your favorite flower?

WATER

Water flows in rivers,

rains, and seas,

God's gentle gift that

brings us peace.

Jesus gives us life,

so pure and clear,

His care refreshes, always near.

God's care gives us life.

Thank You, Jesus, for Your life!

LIGHT

Light glows bright and
chases dark away,
Like Jesus' love,
guiding every day.
When you're scared,
His light will always glow,
Reminding you His love will show.

Jesus is our light.
How does light make you feel safe?

SHADE

Shade cools you when the sun's too hot,

God gives rest in a peaceful spot.

Jesus is your shade, a place to hide,

His care protects you where you abide.

Jesus keeps us safe.

Jesus, thank You for Your shade!

TIME

Clocks tick-tock, with days and
nights so sweet,
God plans your moments,
every beat.
Jesus holds your time
with love so kind,
He's with you always,
peace to find.

God plans our time.
What's your favorite time of day?

PROMISES

God's promises glow like stars above,

Always true,

they're full of love.

Jesus came,

God's promise shining bright,

Loving us forever,

day and night.

God keeps His promises.

Thank You, Jesus, for Your promise!

CHOICES

Choices big and small

we make each day,

God helps us pick His loving way.

Jesus shows us how to

share and care,

His kindness guides us everywhere.

God helps us choose right.

What kind choice did you make today?

COMFORT

When you're sad,

Jesus holds you tight,

His love's a hug

through darkest night.

Like a blanket soft,

so warm and true,

God's comfort wraps around you.

Jesus comforts us.

Jesus, hug me when I'm sad!

THE CROSS

Jesus' cross shows God's
great love for you,
He died and rose,
made all things new.
His cross brings us close
to God above,
Forever wrapped in His endless love!

The cross shows God's love.
Thank You, Jesus, for the cross!

JOY

Joy is God's gift,

making hearts sing,

Laughing, dancing—

praising everything!

Jesus loves our smiles,

so glad and bright,

His joy fills days with happy light.

God gives us joy.

Thank You, Jesus, for joy!

www.ingramcontent.com/pod-product-compliance
Lightning Source LLC
Chambersburg PA
CBHW041411010526
44107CB00015B/1140